Get Into The Zone In Just One Minute

21 Simple Techniques
To Improve Your Performance

2nd Edition

by

Jay P. Granat, Ph.D.

ISBN 978-1-934209-63-9

10-digit ISBN 1-934209-63-5

2nd Edition

Cover design & layout by Christopher Taylor

Edited by M. Stefan Strozier and Kyle David Torke

Published by World Audience, Inc.
303 Park Avenue South
Suite 1440
New York, NY 10010-3657

World Audience Publishers (www.worldaudience.org) is a global consortium of artists and writers, producing the literary journal *audience*, and *The audience Review*. Our periodicals and books are edited by M. Stefan Strozier and assistant editors. Please submit your stories, poems, paintings, and photography to: submissions@worldaudience.org; inquiries about being a reviewer: theatre@worldaudience.org. Thank you.

Get Into The Zone In Just One Minute

by

Jay P. Granat, Ph.D.

A World Audience Book

(www.worldaudience.org)

January, 2009, 2nd Edition

New York (NY, USA)
Newcastle (NSW, Australia)

Dedicated to the thousands of patients who have allowed me to help them, and who have taught me so much about courage, perseverance, tenacity, focus, optimism, playfulness, risk taking, enjoying life, and staying in the zone.

Thanks, Mom.

My mother, Helen Parker, is a retired school teacher. She taught me a lot about writing over the years. I think she did a fairly good job, since I have written several books and hundreds of articles in mainstream publications and in professional journals. Mom, I want to thank you for copy editing this second edition. I also want to thank you for being a supportive parent and for teaching me a lot about mental toughness and about bouncing back from life's challenges. Last, thanks for the delicious chicken soup, the outstanding pot roast and for calling everybody dear and darling when you speak to them.

TABLE OF CONTENTS

What Is Different About This Book?

There are many books and programs on improving your mental outlook and your performance. However, to my knowledge, this is the only manual that teaches you how to get your mind and body into the ideal state in a highly efficient manner and in a very short period of time. Imagine how useful it will be for you to be able to quickly get into the state of mind that will allow you to feel good and to perform to your fullest potential.

Being able to ease your mind into the right gear, as I like to describe it, is an important skill for many people who are trying to excel in today's fast paced and highly competitive society. Learning this skill will be very helpful at work, at sports, at school and even at home.

With a little practice, you will master the simple methods presented in this book. And in just a little while, you will find that you can transport yourself into the zone with increased ease and increased frequency. Some of you will discover that you can get there almost automatically.

Many of my patients now know how to enter the zone quite rapidly. Some can get themselves there in a matter of seconds. Take a moment to consider all of the times in your life when you need to feel good and to perform well. Mastering a method for getting into this mental and physical space can have a profound and deep impact on your life and on the lives of people you love.

So, now you can get ready to get into the zone and stay in the zone. This book shows you how to do it quickly, simply and easily.

Who Can Benefit From Being In The Zone?

For more than twenty years, I have been helping people to feel better, think better and perform better. I have been showing them what they need to do to get into the zone and stay there. My patients have included:

◊ Olympic athletes

◊ professional golfers

◊ football players

◊ professional tennis players

◊ martial artists

◊ professional bowlers

◊ basketball players

◊ swimmers

◊ divers

◊ gymnasts

◊ ice skaters

◊ horse shoe players

◊ pole-vaulters

◊ runners

◊ baseball players

◊ high jumpers

◊ chief executive officers

◊ trial attorneys

◊ racquetball players

◊ skiers

◊ archers

◊ fencers

◊ wrestlers

◊ chess players

◊ scrabble players

◊ poker players

◊ public speakers

◊ salespeople

◊ actors

◊ singers

◊ dancers

◊ artists

◊ firemen

◊ backgammon players

◊ options traders

◊ gold traders

◊ stock traders

◊ bond traders

◊ writers

◊ students preparing for important exams

◊ billiards players

◊ weight lifters

◊ people who play competitive darts

◊ people who compete in equestrian events

◊ a professional bass fisherman

Although I grew up on the streets of Brooklyn, I have even helped professional cowboys who want to perform better in rodeos. One professional cowgirl from Texas told me that I am pretty popular amongst the cowboys on the rodeo circuit. "Dr. Granat, they enjoy listening to your soft voice and your New York accent on your audio programs while they sit in their pick up trucks and get ready to compete in their event," she said.

I had explained to the cowboys that I don't know much about horses, but I do understand what they need to do to get into the right state of mind to be in touch with the animals and compete well.

Similarly, a gymnast who called me on the phone for some coaching explained that she knew my voice. I was not quite certain what she meant until she explained that her coaches play my Stay In The Zone CD while the team practices.

This CD program is available at:

www.stayinthezone.com/get_stay.htm

Many of us are under a lot of pressure and we are all looking for tools and strategies that will help us to perform our best. It does not matter whether you are a professional athlete or a public speaker. Knowing what you need to do to get into the zone can be quite helpful for you, for your career and for your overall well being.

Getting Into The Zone Quickly (Some Real Life Examples)

For more than twenty years, I have been helping people to feel better about themselves and to perform better. Sometimes, the people I counsel are under a lot of pressure and they need techniques, strategies and ideas that will help them in a short period of time. I must have hundreds of examples of interventions that I have used with my patients. In fact, I could probably fill another entire book with these cases.

For now, however, here a few examples of some of the quick solutions that I have used to help people move into the zone. These people use the same methods which are described in detail throughout this guide.

1

A tennis player who I counseled a number of years ago, was quite tense and nervous before his final match. He was the number two seed and he was playing the number one seed who had beaten him many times before. I could not stay for the match because I had to be at a golf tournament with another patient of mine. So, I didn't have the time to talk with the tennis player. Instead, I wrote one of my favorite encouraging remarks on the back of my business card. Here's what I wrote: "Jim, remember, you can never stop the waves, but you can always learn how to surf." This bit of Buddhist philosophy really seemed to resonate with Jim. He stayed calm, focused and he won his match in straight sets. Sometimes, saying the right thing, or in this case, writing an inspiring message can allow a person to develop the attitude they need to feel good and to perform well.

2

A golf pro, who came to see me because he had lost his tempo, needed to rediscover his timing prior to a tournament. In talking to him, I learned that he loved music and that he used to play the guitar. I suggested that he simply get his favorite tune in his head and in his body before he would address the ball. I told him to keep the melody and its rhythm within him throughout his swing. This musical solution helped him to get back on track and finish third in the event.

3

A boxer sought me out because he was not as aggressive in the ring as he wanted to be. This young man loved large, aggressive dogs. I suggested that he start pretending that he was one of his Doberman Pinschers when he stepped through the ropes and into the ring. He pretended he was one of his dogs before his bouts and he found that this idea allowed just the right amount of aggressiveness to emerge.

4

A high school long distance runner had her father call me because she was continually losing in the state finals to the same runner. Her father had been a long distance runner himself, so he was familiar with the mental and physical aspects of competitive running.

The pattern in the previous races was pretty much the same. My client would try to stay close with her nemesis and then during the last lap, she would watch the other woman run away from her. This had happened many times in the past.

I suggested that she go out fast in her next race and try to surprise and shock the other runner. Luckily, this surprise worked. My client won the race after her new and innovative strategy upset the runner who had been beating her regularly.

My client benefited from having a different approach to her sport. This idea freed her up to run harder than she ran in past events. Our battle plan was to force the other runner to catch us for a change. It also allowed my patient to run with greater determination, confidence and intensity than she had in previous races against this young lady.

Sometimes, changing your mental strategy allows you to change the way your body behaves under pressure.

5

About three years ago, I got a call from a male and female duo, who were radio hosts of a morning drive time show in the southern part of the United States. The male member of the team was an avid golfer and he had been a single digit handicap in the past. He called me because he was struggling with his game and he wondered if I could help him via the radio. I thought I could, since I had counseled many people via the phone and e-mail in the past. After talking to the man for quite a while, I had the following advice and suggestions for him.

First, I suggested that he listen to my golf CD program, How To Lower Your Golf Score With Sport Psychology And Self-Hypnosis. This program is available at:

www.stayinthezone.com/we_can_lower_your_score.htm

I recommended that he listen to one chapter a night for a week. I also wanted him to do one other thing, which, at first, he thought was a bit odd.

I told this right handed golfer to practice playing left handed for one week. He did not have to play any rounds. He just had to use a left handed five iron or six iron at the practice range. I had seen this suggestion of playing with your non-dominant side help many of my patients in the past.

The radio host called me after he had followed my suggestions. He told me his last two rounds were back into single digits and he was once again confident on the course.

In some instances, exploring discomfort or "feeling out of the zone," allows us to be able to make contact with the zone.

6

I have used a similar strategy with baseball players who lose confidence in their ability to throw the ball. These players feel that their arm is frozen and they report not being able to get a comfortable feel for the ball. I have had a number of catchers, second baseman and shortstops practice throwing with their non-dominant hand for a week or two. After doing this for a while, they rediscover their confidence and their feel for the baseball.

Again, sometimes, you can find the zone by experiencing what being out of the zone feels like. I occasionally encourage athletes to imagine missing a shot badly. This approach sometimes reawakens their confidence in their shot making. I have used this idea with golfers, basketball players and athletes from many other sports which involve precision and accuracy.

7

I have had right handed baseball hitters hit with their left hand to break out of a hitting slump. Believe it or not, this one idea has cured many hitting slumps.

8

Some time ago, an author who was suffering with a bad case of writer's block asked if I could help him to get the ideas flowing. I placed the man in a light hypnotic trance and I told a rather long story about water falls, streams and currents moving into the ocean. He called me two days later to say that he had written three chapters in his novel. I frequently use inspiring stories, tales, metaphors and anecdotes to unlock, motivate, and inspire people to achieve their goals and to reach their potential.

9

Lots of people who come to me for therapy are in a valley or a slump of some kind. Sometimes I ask them to simply imagine that they are a boxer who is determined to pick himself up from the canvas. This image of the courageous and tenacious fighter inspires many people.

Others respond to the image of a rubber ball that keeps bouncing back no matter what. In fact, the rubber ball bounces higher when it is thrown to the ground with greater force.

10

About a year ago, a diver who wanted to make it to the Olympics came to talk to me. He was not performing well in big meets. I taught him to use a number of the techniques which are included in this book. We also decided that, for him, knowing his competitors' scores was a distraction. Once he decided to not look at the opponents' scores, he was able to dive to his potential.

While some athletes and people like to know where they stand in relation to the competition, others do better performing in a vacuum.

11

A fifty year old golfer came to talk to me, because he wanted to qualify for the senior tour. I placed the man in a deep hypnotic trance and had him imagine and re-experience many of the perfect rounds he had played in the past.

He called me three days later and said, "Doc, we're off to a pretty good start. I just shot a sixty two to tie the course record."

Simply visualizing success in great detail helps many people to find the zone.

12

An eleven year old baseball player who I coached came up to hit in a tense situation. I could see that this talented hitter was quite nervous. I bent down so that we could be at eye level with one another. I looked him in the eyes and told him that I had watched him all season and that I knew that this pitcher threw exactly the kind of stuff that he could hit. He said, "Do you really think so? I told him, "I knew so."

Thirty seconds and two pitches later, he hit a double in the gap to win the game. Sometimes, there is no substitute for a little confidence and knowing that a coach really believes in you.

13

A young ice skater who had taken some nasty falls in competitions came to talk to me to get some help. Her confidence was quite low. Her mind was filled with thoughts of failure.

I taught her how to use self-hypnosis to clear her mind. I told her that she could remove all the negative thoughts just as you would erase words from a blackboard. Her goal was to skate with a clear and clean blackboard or with an empty mind.

Most people do best when their minds are free of all clutter.

14

A baseball pitcher who had lost his focus came to see me for some help. I placed the man in a rather deep hypnotic trance and told him a story about a patient of mine who was a very skilled neurosurgeon. I emphasized the man's excellent, vision, focus and his meticulous nature. These qualities and traits were absorbed by the pitcher and he began to think about the surgeon before the start of every inning. In fact, he viewed himself as a surgeon on the mound. He told me that he was now quite focused and confident when he faced batters.

15

As you might expect, lots of people who want to talk to me are struggling with nervousness, tension or anxiety. Now, telling them not too worry, or to calm down, usually does not help very much.

However, teaching them some simple breathing techniques and providing them with an image that has some meaning for them really does help many of these individuals to feel calmer, enter the zone and perform better.

Two years ago, a physician who was studying for a board exam came to talk to me. I trained him to imagine that his body was in a warm bath while he was taking the exam. This simple technique helped this doctor to pass this important test.

Some time ago, I developed a program for people who suffer from test anxiety or who are nervous about exams. This CD program is available at: www.ConquerTestAnxiety.com.

How To Use This Book

For many years, I have been observing and encouraging large and small mental shifts in people. Sometimes, people want and need a small change in their attitude, routine, behavior, understanding or daily ritual to enter the zone and to have a more fulfilling life. Others need to make large shifts or changes like moving to a different part of the world, changing careers, changing jobs, ending toxic relationships, starting new and healthy relationships, letting go of anger, sadness and depression, minimizing anxiety, ending an addiction, repairing a damaged relationship or healing from an emotional or physical trauma.

For many people, big changes sometimes start with small, incremental changes. Think about how you learned to walk, to ride a bike or to read and write. Most likely, you went through a series of small steps to master the mental and physical skills associated with these tasks.

Mental shifts can give rise to new learning, and to better ways of behaving, feeling, perceiving, dreaming and reacting. For me and for many of my patients, meditation, self-hypnosis, visualization and guided imagery have acted as powerful catalysts for these kinds of changes. Many of the techniques described in this book are a combination of these aforementioned modalities.

Now some of my colleagues like to debate whether meditation, self-hypnosis, hypnosis, visualization or guided imagery are similar or different. I tend to view them as being branches of the same tree and I use all of them with my patients. Consequently, this book includes techniques which are derived from all of these psychological techniques.

As you will discover, there are several components to the zone and we all get there a little differently. This book outlines some simple techniques that I have used with thousands of patients. Each technique is intended to help you to add and delete whatever you need to in order to move yourself into this pleasant and useful state of mind.

Now, I don't know which technique will work best for you, but you can definitely discover which exercise or which combinations of exercises will be most powerful for you.

Read through the whole book leisurely, and go through all of the exercises, one at a time. As you try each exercise, some will resonate more with you than do others. The ones that you like the most probably hold the keys for you to discover and enter the zone more often.

You can feel free to use one approach or you can mix and match several approaches. And you will probably be quite amazed at the benefits of integrating just one or two of these techniques into your daily life.

After counseling thousands of patients during many years of practice, I have observed that very often a simple technique or idea can have a powerful impact on a person. This book contains many simple ideas that have helped lots of people just like you.

Many of you will discover that you are sleeping better, concentrating better, focusing better, performing better and feeling better, once you begin to practice these simple techniques on a regular basis. Lots of you will feel less anxious and less depressed and your stress level will decrease. Many people report feeling more centered, more concentrated and more motivated to take on life's challenges.

I have had many patients who report fantastic results after utilizing the techniques in this book, just one time.

One man cured himself of his chocolate addiction. Another woman got over her fear of flying. A long jumper increased his longest jump by a foot. A person who was afraid of public speaking started doing stand up comedy.

A man with a fear of flying got his pilot's license.

Another advantage to these techniques is that there are no dangerous side effects associated with this kind of approach. That is, these techniques do not contain the dangerous side effects that are associated with some psychotropic medications.

There is no loss of control or consciousness. Instead, you will start to feel that you have greater control over your emotions, your thoughts, your mind and your body.

These benefits will be useful when you need to create an excellent performance, but the skills, I teach you and the feelings and behaviors that accompany them, can have a positive impact on many aspects of your life.

At the end of the book, I list the steps you can go through to enter the zone by using all or most of the techniques described in this guide in one succinct exercise.

I have also included a few narratives that some of you might enjoy using for feeling better and for getting into the zone.

Some individuals feel that they move into a deeper trance state when they employ the longer exercise and they feel this state of mind helps them to discover the zone more effectively.

The longer technique is a compilation of some of the shorter exercises described throughout this book.

If you want to learn more about strategies and techniques for managing stress and for getting into the zone, please visit www.StayInTheZone.com.

For those of you who like listening to audio programs for self-improvement, there is a two CD, twenty chapter program for getting into the zone on this site. Here is the link to get this program: www.stayinthezone.com/get_stay.htm

There is also a three CD program on stress management. This program addresses issues like insomnia, anger management and finding meaning in your life.

Here is the link to get this program:

www.stayinthezone.com/conquer_stress.htm

Can You Really Get Into The Zone In Just One Minute?

The answer is yes.

Now it may take a little time to learn the specific tool or technique that works for you. But over the years, I have been amazed how facilitating a small change in a person's thinking, attitude, feeling or perception can give rise to quick and significant changes.

Many times, patients come back to me and say things like this: "Just learning how to relax had a huge impact on my performance."

"You got me smiling out there and that made all the difference."

"I always dream a big dream the night before I play. This helps to have a goal that motivates me."

"I am not afraid to fail anymore. Getting over that fear helped me to feel much better about myself."

"Once I rediscovered my inner confidence, everything was different."

"I see how my mind impacts my body. When I think positive thoughts, my whole body feels differently and behaves differently."

"I can get myself into the zone really quickly now. I know how to use my imagination to get there."

"When I first came to see you, my mind was always racing with many thoughts. Now I can fill my mind with just one idea."

"I simply erase all negative thoughts whenever they try to sneak into my brain. That's all I need to do to enter the zone."

"I find something to smile about and everything changes for me."

"I start the day with my favorite exercise and then I do it again a few times a day. That exercise changes the way I think and feel right away."

These quotes are from people who are using the same simple and brief techniques described in this book. If these methods can help them, they can help you too.

Experiment a bit and put in a little time and you will discover your quick pathway to the zone.

What Is The Zone?

Many people who come to see me want to get into the zone. Interestingly, some of these people are a bit unclear as to what the zone really is. Some of this confusion is easy to understand, since the zone has been described differently by different writers and researchers. My definition is based on interviews with hundreds of athletes who have been in the zone and out of the zone.

I have expanded and modified the definition over the years. At this point, I think I have a rather comprehensive explanation of this mental state.

The zone is a state of mind which is marked by a sense of calmness. In addition, there is a heightened sense of awareness and focus. In this state of mind, there is no self-criticism and the person is living in the present. They are immersed in the here and now. Actions seem effortless and there is an increased belief that your dreams or goals can become achievable and real. In addition, there is also a sense of deep enjoyment when the person is in this unique, special and magical state of being.

As you probably can tell, this is a very enjoyable state of mind.

In my view, the zone is an altered state of consciousness that closely parallels a trance state or a hypnotic state of mind. This book teaches you how to incorporate all of the elements of the zone into your mind and your body by using a combination of self-hypnosis, visualization, meditation, guided imagery, positive thinking, and common sense.

What Does The Zone Really Feel Like?

My patients have described the zone in many different ways.

A baseball player said, "Everything is easy. The ball seems huge. I know what the pitcher is throwing before he releases the ball. I feel great. It's a high. These good feelings extend beyond the baseball diamond. As a matter of fact, my sex life even improves when I feel like I'm in the zone."

A football lineman told me, "The guys on the other side of the ball look smaller."

A hockey goalie said, "I feel bigger and quicker in the net."

A golfer claimed, "I feel like I am the ball. I don't have to think about a thing. It just happens."

A boxer described it this way, "I can anticipate the punches before they leave my opponent's body. My reactions are faster. This gives me a big edge in the ring."

A trial attorney said, "I am prepared and ready and when I get in front of the jury, there is no doubt in my mind about my ability to persuade them. I stay in the moment and I present my case with ease and confidence. My thinking is clear and I am enjoying the spotlight."

A chess player told me, "I see the board, the pieces and the geometry of the game very clearly."

A scrabble player explained, "The words start to jump out at me without having to work hard or think about it too hard. It's like I discover this dictionary within me."

"It was like a wonderful dream on ice. It was me, my skates, the ice and the music," according to a figure skater I counseled.

A downhill skier had this description of the zone:

"I was connected with nature in a way that I had never been before. I was racing down that mountain at top speed, but it felt like I was traveling in slow motion. It was unbelievable."

"I was playing in a bubble. It was the ball, the court, me and him. There was a huge crowd, but I did not notice them at all." These were the remarks of a tennis pro at a large tournament.

A professional bowler who used my Stay In The Zone CD program said, "When I step on the lane, I have just one thought in my mind. I clear my head of everything but that one idea."

An actor said, "I didn't have to think about a thing. I was totally absorbed in my role and I felt that special connection between myself and the audience. It felt like everything was slow and easy. I lost track of time during that performance."

A long distance runner described the zone this way. "I felt like everything was on automatic pilot. My legs felt light and so did my body. It seemed like I could run forever, even though I had been running for more than ninety minutes."

A basketball player said, "My normal shooting range is fifteen to twenty feet. When I was in the zone, I felt like I could sink shots from thirty feet. The hoop seemed larger and I knew the ball was going to drop before it left my hands."

Now, you cannot force your way into the zone. You need to ease your way in. This book will teach you the key steps that you need to take to move your mind and your body into the zone. With some practice, you will find that you can get yourself to this destination with more and more frequency and with greater ease.

As I noted earlier, I have been practicing these mental exercises for many years and I and I can alter my mood, my self-confidence and my focus in a minute. With practice, you, too, will be able to change the way you think, feel, and behave, quickly and efficiently.

Barriers From Entering The Zone

To better understand what it is like to be in the zone, it is important to understand what being out of the zone is like. If you dissect the definition, you can see the kinds of mental factors which will block you from entering the zone. So, if you are nervous or anxious, you cannot enter the zone. If you are self-critical, you won't get into the zone. If you are living in the past or the future as opposed to the here and now, you will not get into the zone. If you are thinking about your physical actions, you can not ease yourself into the zone. If you are angry, bored or not having fun at what you are doing, you will not be able to transport your mind and your body into the zone. If you're distracted by many different stimuli, you can't develop the singular focus that is a prerequisite for entering the zone.

It is also useful if you know what your dreams, fantasies and goals are since having this knowledge can help you to maintain your focus and your relaxed concentration.

Your "Out Of The Zone" Experience

Sometimes, you have to determine and sort out what is wrong or problematic in order to solve a problem. When I give workshops or when I counsel clients, I frequently suggest that they write an out of the zone essay and then an "in the zone" essay.

When people are feeling like they are out of the zone, they say some interesting, insightful and revealing things.

For example, a tennis player said, "My mind was racing. I couldn't settle myself down and my legs felt like rubber."

A chief executive officer of a large company felt like he was out of the zone when he delivered a speech to his top managers. "I felt very nervous.

I think the people in the audience sensed it. My ideas just wouldn't flow. I really bombed that day."

A baseball pitcher described his out of the zone experience this way. "The ball just didn't feel right in my hands. I could never get comfortable on the mound."

A golfer couldn't shut off his negative thoughts in a big tournament. He told me, "I kept thinking about how poorly I played this course last year. I couldn't get that score of eighty five out of my mind."

A basketball player said that his arm felt like it was made out of cement when he had to make some key free throws at the end of a game.

A baseball player in a hitting slump remarked, "I am great in batting practice and great when I face the machine. But when a big game begins, I just can't get loose and can't seem to find my confidence."

This first piece of writing will help you to identify what is blocking you from getting into the zone and from performing better and feeling better.

Take some time to write at least two hundred and fifty words describing your out of the zone experience. This might be a time that choked or a time you felt you performed poorly. It can be a sporting event, a sales presentation, a speech or an exam. It can be an old event or something recent. Feel free to write several essays, if you are inclined to do so. The more you understand about what allows you to exit and enter the zone— the better. Underline the key feelings, thoughts, ideas and sensations which you associate with the zone.

_____

_____

_____

_____

_____

_____

_____

Your "In The Zone" Experience

Now write two hundred and fifty words about your zone experience. You will probably find this to be quite enjoyable and quite informative. Underline the key sensations, feelings, memories and thoughts which you connect with being in the zone.

_____

_____

_____

_____

_____

_____

_____

_____

_____

Now review both of your essays and underline the key words, phrases, images and feelings. Some of you have probably recalled specific physical and mental sensations that you connect with these states. Many of you will be surprised at the great detail you were able to recall about these experiences.

You can also probably identify very clearly how your mind felt and how your body felt during these high and low points of your life.

In my office, I have people sit in a chair that we designate as "the out of the zone" seat. And then, I have them sit in the "in the zone" seat. This exercise helps people experience, differentiate and sense what is different about these contrasting states of mind. I have them describe the different feelings in great detail.

The out of the zone experience almost always includes tension, anxiety, self-doubt, self-criticism, worries about the futures, regrets about the past, too much thinking, an abundance of negative self-talk, a lack of confidence, poor focus, a myriad of distractions and poor performances.

As you can see, this is the polar opposite of what the zone is.

If you like, you can try the two chair exercise on your own. You can simply read your out of the zone essay in your out of the zone chair, and then read your in the zone essay in your zone seat. Notice carefully what happens with your body and your feelings as your describe both states.

This technique will help you to better determine what you need to focus on when you go through the method which I will outline a little later in this book.

Choking-----
The Zone

Another way to think about the zone is to consider its opposite. Athletes sometimes refer to this as choking. When you choke, the wheels come off. You can't seem to handle the pressure of the situation or the moment. You lose your confidence, your composure, your focus and your will ability to perform to your potential.

It is important for you to understand that everyone chokes sometimes. After all, you are a human being, not a machine.

Now, I cannot teach you how to get into the zone all the time. This is impossible. However, I can show you how to move your mind and your body from the choking state of mind towards the zone.

Frequently, a simple mental shift allows people to make this transition and get themselves back on track.

A smile, a mantra, an idea, an image, a joke, a lucky medallion, a prayer, a coach, a new thought, a new plan, a song, a dream or a memory can terminate a choking state and ease a person back into the zone.

Left Brain-----
Right Brain

Another way to think about the zone is to view it primarily as right brain experience. So, you can think of entering the zone as being a way of waking up or activating this part of your mind. I don't believe that the left brain is not at all active in the zone, but it appears that this is largely a right brain experience.

Left Brain Functions

- ♠ uses logic
- ♠ detail oriented
- ♠ facts rule
- ♠ words and language
- ♠ present and past
- ♠ math and science
- ♠ can comprehend
- ♠ knowing
- ♠ acknowledges
- ♠ order/pattern perception
- ♠ knows object name
- ♠ reality based
- ♠ forms strategies
- ♠ practical
- ♠ safe

Right Brain Functions

- ♣ uses feeling
- ♣ "big picture" oriented
- ♣ imagination rules
- ♣ symbols and images
- ♣ present and future
- ♣ philosophy & religion
- ♣ can "get it" (i.e. meaning)
- ♣ believes
- ♣ appreciates
- ♣ spatial perception
- ♣ knows object function
- ♣ fantasy based
- ♣ presents possibilities
- ♣ impetuous
- ♣ risk taking

How Did I Get Interested In The Zone?

As a young boy, I observed some martial artists who were accomplishing some amazing tasks. I saw people break bricks and boards using their hands, their feet and their heads. I was awestruck when I saw a martial arts master stop the flow of blood from a self-inflicted wound.

As a matter of fact, when I was being trained in hypnosis and hypnotherapy, I was able to train my mind to control the number of drops that I bled from two small punctures in the back of my hand.

I placed myself in a trance, in a zone like state and I concentrated intensively on the number seven and sure enough I bled a total of seven drops and then the bleeding stops.

When I told my wife this story, she was quite surprised that I volunteered this demonstration, since I tend to avoid hospitals and medical procedures as much as possible.

As I grew older and played a variety of different sports, I became increasingly more curious as to why I could go four for four in baseball one day and why I could go zero for four the following day.

Why could I bowl a two hundred and twenty game and follow it with a one hundred and sixty game?

On some days I could make what seemed like every basketball shot I would take and on other days I couldn't seem to hit the side of a barn with the round ball.

48

Why was this? And what could be done to help me to train my mind to help my body to perform to its fullest potential?

Once I became a therapist, I remained curious and fascinated by mind-body relationships. Early in my career, I counseled overweight and obese patients at a hospital.

Clearly, many of the people had minds and bodies which were quite out of balance with one another.

Once I learned hypnosis, meditation and visualization techniques, I knew these powerful tools and techniques could be helpful to many people.

I Use Techniques
Described In This Book
All The Time

Several months ago, I was asked to appear on Canadian National Television. The journalist who called me asked if I would debate a man who had an opposing viewpoint to mine on a rather controversial and politically charged issue which was receiving a lot of media attention at the time.

I agreed to appear. I was not feeling anxious or nervous at all until I got into the studio. I had been on television before, so that was not the issue that was bothering me.

There were a few things that were different this time. A live debate in front of millions of viewers would be a new experience, as would the idea of talking to a split screen and listening to my adversary and the moderators through an ear piece.

While I was waiting for the broadcast to start, I felt myself getting a bit nervous. My heart was racing a bit and my palms were a little sweaty.

To calm myself, maintain my focus and my confidence, I used three or four of the techniques that I describe in this book.

Each one of them took about a minute to implement: I used my breathing to calm myself down. I viewed the experience from a playful and curious perspective and I focused very carefully on the ideas and thoughts that I wanted to communicate.

I did not dwell on the size of the audience. I knew that could be intimidating. Instead, I focused on my strength which was my knowledge of the subject matter and my ability to communicate about it.

Based on the audience feedback, I think I did pretty well. So, you see, I am conveying to you tools and strategies that work for myself as well for my clients and patients. I strongly and sincerely believe in this approach. If you are open minded, I think you will find them to be quite valuable as well.

My Kids Use These Techniques Too

Last month, my twelve year old son was playing in his third or fourth tennis tournament. Prior to the start of the matches, he came over to me and said, "Daddy I don't feel so good. I can't breathe and I am really nervous."

I told him that he came to talk to the right person. I suggested that he make all the muscles in his body really tense and then count to ten. When he reached ten, he was instructed to relax his muscles.

I then gave him a big hug and kiss and I told him I was here if he needed anything else from me. I also reminded him that I loved him very much, no matter what happened in the tournament.

He did what I suggested a few times, although he was looking at me like I was a bit crazy as he went through the exercises.

After the first match, he came up to tell me that my idea really worked and he thanked me for the help.

My daughter is a talented singer. Before a recent performance, she was a bit nervous. I asked her to remember how great she felt when she really let her voice really go at a previous concert. When I saw that she was absorbed in the memory of that wonderful musical experience, I encouraged her to share her beautiful and powerful voice with people once again.

She entered the zone and wowed a very large audience with a few difficult songs.

Your kids might benefit from learning these techniques too. In my experience, children really enjoy this kind of mental training. These skills can help them in their school life and in their athletic life. Moreover, learning these skills early can help your kids throughout their adult lives.

Discovering Another Part Of Your Mind

Early on in my practice, when I was quite naïve about human nature, I became quite frustrated with patients who, for some reason, would not follow logic or listen to reason. This unwillingness or inability to accept logic and reason presented itself in many patients.

For example, I had counseled hundreds of attractive, capable and charming people who were remaining in abusive and toxic relationships, even though they knew these situations were poisonous for their well being.

Likewise, I had treated thousands of overweight patients who knew they were harming themselves, but could not seem to take charge of their minds and their bodies.

I tried everything I could think of to motivate and to help these patients, but frankly, I was having little success.

In my own life, I was struggling with some demons from the past and traditional kinds of therapy did not seem to be helping me either. I had seen a myriad of therapists and I did not feel like I was feeling any better or doing any better in my life.

I was kind of stuck and I felt that too many of my patients were stuck too.

I reasoned that there had to be another way to get through to people and to get my own life on a better path.

Luckily, I discovered techniques like hypnosis, self-hypnosis, meditation and visualization which changed my life and allowed me to help many people who I could not help with logic and with psychotherapeutic techniques which were based primarily on cognitive-behavioral methods.

I found a whole new way to change my own way of thinking, feeling, behaving and perceiving the world and myself. I communicated with my patients in a brand new way and I felt like I was now having a huge impact on many people's lives in a short period of time.

I was helping them to change in ways that there logical minds would not allow them to do. I was now communicating with their unconscious minds, their right brains, their imaginations and their inner guides. I was getting through to the part of them that can imagine new ways of being.

Many of the techniques in this book are derived from my experience and training in hypnosis, self-hypnosis, visualization, guided imagery and meditation. If you have never had any training in these techniques, you are in for an eye-opening and mind opening treat. If you are experienced in these methods, you will probably find some new, simple and effective ways to build on the skills you already have developed.

Okay, now that you know a little about the zone and me and how this book works, we can get started with some of the actual techniques. It's time to ease your mind and your body and start your pleasant journey into the zone.

Enjoy Your
Favorite Music

Many books that talk about self-hypnosis, meditation, visualization or relaxation training begin with a procedure which many newcomers to this mental training find to be somewhat complicated and a bit difficult to master. I am a big believer in teaching people simple skills first and then moving on to more advanced techniques.

In fact, some of you may already be using these techniques on your own. We are simply formalizing them a bit and reminding you of some the ways that you can use what you are already doing to shift your mind and your body into an ideal performance state.

Almost everybody can quickly master the first few techniques that I will teach you here. The first involves something you already probably use to unwind and to change your mood-music.

When I teach people how to enter the zone, I frequently include music in the process.

I usually ask the person if they like music, and so far no one has told me that they don't enjoy some form of music.

In my view, nothing can change a person's mood more quickly than their favorite tunes can. Play one of your favorite songs and notice how your mind and your mind change in a positive way in a matter of seconds. Music is also a great way of waking up your right brain which I discussed earlier in this book.

Now, you don't have to use new age music. You can use anything that you enjoy.

And you don't have to use music at all to enter the zone. Some people report that they find songs to be a bit distracting. And there will be times when you want to enter the zone, but you don't have access to your favorite music. Although, with I-Pods, cell phones and MP 3 players, this is a bit hard to imagine happening these days.

However, you can always try singing, whistling or humming your favorite music. You are never without your imagination. And you can always put your mind and your memory of music to work for you. And some of your purists will want to create your own music without using any technology. If you play an instrument, you know that it is a wonderful and simple way to adjust your mood and calm an anxious, sad, lethargic, racing or worried mind.

Again, you can use any music you like. Some of my patients love classical or opera. Some find that a sad, blues tune helps them to feel better. Others rely on rock and roll or rap music to find their right energy level. As for me, I prefer I prefer Motown. Motown's energy and its rhythm work great for me. Plus, those tunes bring back some wonderful memories of my youth.

Believe it or not, one minute of your favorite music can move your mind, your body and your spirit into the zone. Give it a try or combine music with any of the other techniques in this book that you enjoy.

Smile

Find something to smile about. Perhaps you enjoy a joke of the day. Maybe, you like to reminisce about something you did in your youth. I wonder if you can recall something that your child did that brought a warm smile to your face.

Maybe you like to revisit an early mischievous or intimate experience. Call a friend with a good sense of humor. Recall an anecdote that causes you to laugh really hard. Reflect on the silliest or dumbest thing you have ever done.

I once changed the wrong tire. I was late for an exam and I was quite anxious. Talk about being out of the zone. I changed what I thought was the right tire. I threw the jack into the trunk of my car. After driving perhaps twenty yards, I realized what I had done. Boy, did I feel stupid. Tension and anxiety can really short circuit your brain. I did get to class in time for the exam, and as it turned out, I, somehow, managed to get a very good grade on the test. Fortunately, the professor wasn't testing me on my tire changing skills or my mechanical abilities.

I frequently share a humorous anecdote with patients in my office and I often tell highly competitive athletes a humorous story before a very important competition.

Very often, the key thing is to bring some laughter, levity or a smile into your consciousness.

Music, which was discussed in the last chapter, and laughter are simple and great triggers for changing your mood and for entering the zone. Some of you will have success entering the zone by using one or both of these approaches.

Think how simple it is to listen to your favorite song and then to just recall a humorous event or anecdote. Try this right now and you will see how you start to feel differently in a very short period of time.

Focus

As I mentioned at the start of this book, focus is a vital part of the zone experience.

So, let's begin this technique by having you find something in your wallet, or your room, or your office or your pocketbook that has special meaning for you. This can be a photo, a piece of jewelry, a crystal, a stone, a key or a watch. It really does not matter what you choose. Just select something that you like or love and something that you have positive associations with.

Hold the object in your non-dominant hand and enjoy it. Notice how it feels and what happens to you as you get absorbed in this item.

Take note of its weight, its texture, how it feels in your hand and how your mind and your body change a bit as you get absorbed in this exercise and this item. Notice if you gravitate toward a part of the object or if you enjoy observing the entire object.

You will see that as your focus shifts that your feelings and thoughts change as well. You discover that you can tune out distractions and release negative or uncomfortable thoughts without having to try to do so. And, you feel a little differently than you did just a moment ago. Concentrating on just one thing can move you into a comfortable meditative like state of mind.

By the way, if you don't want to use an object you can use something you always have with you like your right fist. You can simply make a comfortable fist and focus all of your attention on it. Observe its weight, its power, its texture and how it feels and how it looks to you.

This focusing exercise is quite helpful for people who are easily distracted.

And as I mentioned earlier, the zone involves some sense of focus. So, eliminating or minimizing distraction can be quite useful in your quest to enter the zone.

Stay In The Here And Now

One of the major barriers to getting into the zone involves thinking too much about the past or too much about the present. Interestingly, depressed people tend to be reliving their past regrets. Anxious people seem to negatively project into the future.

To enter the zone, however, you have to learn to release the past and let go of self-criticism for what you would have done, could have done, would have done or should have done.

Those events are history. Perhaps you can learn from them, but you can not change them. They don't have to be alive or relevant now.

Similarly, you need to let go of your fear about what negative event or undesirable outcome might occur in the next minute, day, week or month.

I once heard that the only fears that we are born with are the fears of height and of loud noises. The rest of our fears and anxieties about the future are learned by us.

It stands to reason then that many of our fears about the terrible things that might happen to us can be unlearned or at least managed more effectively.

In fact, many, if not all, of these things we worry about will probably never happen. I think you can see the value of staying in the present and how this present orientation is an important part of entering the zone.

The previous techniques described in this book should help many of you to stay in the present. However, if you need a little more assistance with this mental skill, try focusing on the second hand of a watch or a clock. And as you gaze at the hand moving one second at a time, zero in that and nothing else. If your mind strays, or moves forward in time or back in time, ground yourself by guiding your mind to the second hand.

And this is all you need to be concerned with right now. You are in a cocoon of the present where you can forget about the past and let go of any negative concerns, thoughts or fears about what might happen and about the future.

As you zero in on the second hand, you will notice that you experience a number of interesting and pleasant physical and mental changes. This is a great way centering yourself and of tuning distractions which have nothing to do with the all important here and now of the zone.

By the way, you can link this technique with the previous strategies mentioned in this guide. So, listen to music, find something to smile about, pick up a favorite object and move your mind into the present. Some of you will feel that you have already moved into the zone.

A Simple Way To Relax
Your Mind

It is hard, if not impossible, to feel good and accomplish anything if you are tense or anxious. So, you need to find a way to calm down and relax. Now most of us can't do this by telling ourselves to calm down. But you can do it by retraining your mind. One of the fastest and easiest ways to relax is to simply close your eyes and take a few deep breaths. Be sure to breathe deeply enough to feel your belly expand and contract. And breathe easily, deeply and gently taking air in through your nose and releasing it out of your mouth. If you're doing this right, your jaw will separate and you will find a comfortable pace for your breathing.

And as you breathe in relaxation, joy, calmness, hope and optimism. You can release any anxiety, self doubt, self-criticism, tension or negativity that you may be within you as you breathe out.

And as you enjoy this calmness and peace, you can say the word "tranquility" to yourself over and over again. And you can imagine the word "tranquility" written, printed or painted on any sign, or screen or poster that you like.

And you will notice that closing your eyes, breathing deeply, and attending to the word "tranquility" changes the way you feel. Doesn't it? And this is all you need to do to relax at any time and at any place. Use this technique by itself or use it in conjunction with any of the other methods outlined in this book. (I use this one several times a day.)

If you like, you can begin with relaxation and then move to *focus* or *smile* or to your *music*. Some people need the formal relaxation training to then use the music or the smile. Others can begin in a different manner.

You will need to experiment a bit.

You can also use your breathing to let go of anger and frustration. These toxic feelings will definitely block you from finding the zone. If you can't completely eliminate anger and frustration just yet, try to reduce these feelings a bit. Try to release them as you exhale and replace them with peace, gentleness and patience.

In time, and with a little regular practice, you will be able to diminish these feelings significantly or manage them in a healthier way. (If, anger and frustration are big issues for you, you may want to consider using the Stay In The Zone CD program. It has a chapter devoted to managing anger and frustration.)

Here is the link to get that program:

www.stayinthezone.com/get_stay.htm

How To Relax Your Body In One Minute

Now that you know how to relax your mind, you can turn your attention to your body. Start by making two tight fists and keeping your hands, fingers, wrists, arms, forearms and upper arms tense for twenty seconds. Count slowly from one to twenty. Then relax your hands let them go limp and notice the real physical difference between tension and relaxation.

You can repeat this tensing and relaxation exercise several times if you like and you do a similar exercise with all or with any of the muscles of your body.

To intensify your feelings of relaxation, you can imagine that you are experiencing a warm bath, a massage, time in a sauna or a steam bath or a nap on your favorite couch, hammock or beach blanket.

You will be amazed at how easily your mind can recreate this experience and how your body can feel the physiological changes that go along with relaxing and peaceful images.

If you tend to hold a lot of tension in your body, you may want this exercise to be the first one you use to enter the zone. Then, you can add on any of the other ones that you enjoy and find useful.

For many athletes, a relaxed body is essential for entering the zone and for delivering a fine performance. Some find that all they need to find the zone is a relaxed body. Their minds tend to follow, once they feel physically peaceful.

However, I have one word of caution where this technique is concerned. Some of you may find that this technique can get you too relaxed. You may feel a bit flat or lethargic and this can work against you, if your zone performance requires some energy and exuberance.

As I will explain a little later on in this book, discovering your right energy level is another vital factor for getting into the zone.

Move Your Mind Down The Right Path

Almost every day, you are faced with some kind of emotional crossroad. You have a choice as to whether you want to allow your mind to go down the negative path or the positive one. The negative path is loaded with self-doubt, self-criticism, pessimism, regrets, anxiety, lack of confidence and the kind of self-talk that will take you out of the zone and most likely lead to disappointment.

When you feel your mind is headed toward that negative path, ease your brain back onto a more positive way of thinking. Realize that it is very normal to experience self-doubt from time to time. The trick is to not allow yourself to be consumed by this kind of thinking.

Try to focus on the flowers instead of the weeds when you look at the garden that makes up your life.

Try to view every problem as an opportunity to grow and learn rather than as a crisis.

If you are facing a dark experience, try to light a candle.

Keeping your mind on a positive path will definitely help you to stay in the zone.

Take A Mental Vacation

Some of you will want to intensify your relaxation experience, by allowing your mind to move to your favorite place. For many of you, this will be the beach. Most of us like the water, the sand, the waves, watching people walking by, taking a walk yourself, exploring the jetty, checking out the water, laying in the sun, listening to the seagulls, doing a little fishing or eating some fresh seafood. Kids like to pick up shells and play in the sand. And you might like this too. There is certainly a lot to enjoy at the beach.

Others might like the woods. That contact with trees, soil, grass, rocks and lakes changes the way you feel and the way you think. Hiking up a trail or walking up and down a grassy valley can cause you to breathe differently, and feel quite differently than you felt a few moments ago.

Some of you may enjoy a walk in the park or a stroll in the city.

When you spend time in your favorite surroundings, you tend to think differently and feel differently. You tend to let go of negative feelings and you discover that your critical inner voice, an important barrier from entering the zone, is quieter and less obtrusive.

So visit your favorite place and enjoy all that you love about the spot. The feelings, memories, sensations and thoughts that you associate with this place can give you some clues as to what will help you get into the zone.

Make Contact
With Nature

A connection with nature seems to have a positive impact on most of us. I love to pet my dogs and swim in the ocean. You might enjoy gardening or raking leaves or hiking in the woods. Maybe you love a day of fishing in the ocean or in a beautiful stream. Some make contact with nature when they run or walk. Others like capturing the essence and feelings of nature through art, photography or sculpture. Skin diving and snorkeling is another fantastic way to reconnect with Mother Nature. Surfing, snowboarding and skiing are some other great ways to get these feelings. An outdoor concert on a beautiful night can be another fantastic vehicle for changing your mood and altering your consciousness in a way that is compatible with getting into the zone.

You can re-experience your closeness to Mother Nature by using your imagination or your right brain to review all that you love about the outdoors, animals, plants, the ocean, lakes, rivers, streams, a roaring camp fire, old trees, a brilliant sky, a rainbow, a sunset or a sunrise.

One of my patients is a photographer who lives in New York City. He takes a daily walk in Central Park and he notices that his mood changes significantly the moment he enters the park and sees the trees, the dogs running and the children playing. He feels that he finds his best photographs after he leaves the park. I suspect he makes meaningful contact with nature during his walk and that enters the zone after his stroll.

Interestingly, many people report having better vision when they are in the zone. I have heard this from golfers and baseball players and others whose performance relies on seeing clearly. I wonder if this is true for this man who earns his living by taking photographs.

How To Build Your Confidence *Quickly*

As I mentioned earlier, confidence is an important part of the zone. So, now I want to introduce you to a two part technique which will allow you to build your confidence and enable you to enter the zone feeling good about yourself.

Now that you know how to relax your mind and your body, and you know how to guide your mind into a comfortable spot, I want you to use your imagination to do something a little different.

I want you to recall one person in your life who you love or loved very much. And this person felt very strongly about you too.

This may have been your mom or your dad, an aunt, an uncle, a coach, a friend, a sibling, a teacher or a neighbor. But this person made your feel very special. They looked at you in a loving way and they said some wonderful things to you that you have never forgotten.

You remember what this person looks like, sounds like, smells like and you recall very clearly what it feels like to be hugged by this man or woman. They are very special. This person is your inner coach. Have this special individual stay with you and accompany you as you ease into the zone.

Take their message with you and keep them close by.

(If you recall, someone who you have not seen in a while or who has died, you may experience some sadness when you use this technique. That can be okay, because your sadness signals that they were very special and they you loved them very much and they probably felt the same way about you. If your sadness becomes a problem, I suggest that you choose another special person as your inner coach on this mental journey. Or, you may find it too upsetting, in which case, you probably should skip this exercise.)

For those of you who want to continue, simply read on.

Now that your inner coach is with you, I want you to recall in great detail a time in your life when you felt great about yourself. Perhaps you accomplished something physical. Maybe, you did well on an exam. Maybe, you discovered something or solved a complicate problem. Recall this wonderful event in great detail and with great clarity. You can probably visualize what you were wearing back then. Some of you will remember exactly what you looked like at this time in your life.

And even though you haven't thought about it for a long time, you can vividly remember how wonderful you felt back then and you can re-experience all those super feelings, thoughts, ideas and sensations once again.

Some of you will find it interesting to revisit something you accomplished a long time ago like riding a bike, learning to read, to write or to walk.

Recalling these early experiences can teach you something about being resilient, persistent, hopeful and optimistic. They can also remind you what self-confidence feels like to you.

And, remember, self-confidence is an integral part of the getting into the zone. If you like, you can easily add this technique to some of the others described in this guide. Or, you can use this one on its own. This one has been a favorite with many of my patients.

Dream A Glorious And Wonderful Dream

And now that you are feeling relaxed and more confident, it is time to let yourself dream, imagine and wonder. And, wonder what you would really like to do with this relaxed feeling, and this increased sense of empowerment.

You can pretend you are your favorite hero. You can imagine that you are handling a situation the way your mentor might manage it. You can be a star, a champion and expert.

Just act as if you have arrived.

You can set as big a goal for yourself as you want to. Or, you can pick a small change that you want to make. You don't have to rush to do it all at once.

But imagine succeeding at something or learning something that you have always wanted to do. Or, if you prefer, revisit something that you have enjoyed in the past.

Remember, you become what you think. So, take this time and this opportunity to imagine something really special for yourself.

Some of you will enjoy using a variation of this technique to influence what you are likely to dream about before you go to sleep. Here's how to do it. Go through the exercise described above and then write down what you would like to dream about before you go to sleep. Many of you will be amazed at how you can shape the content of your dreams.

Some of you will get some interesting information from your dream the first time you try this exercise. Others will find that it might take a week or two to have a dream which his related to the issue you wanted to explore while you sleep.

Give this experiment a try. Many people find that their dreams give them great insight into what they need to do to get into the zone more often.

Discover Your Right Energy Level

Another important component of your zone experience is knowing your optimal energy level. A boxer needs a different kind of energy than does a professional golfer. Likewise, some people deliver effective speeches in a relaxed and easy going style, while others like a more high energy and vibrant approach.

I don't know if you like to drive at fifty five miles per hour or at seventy miles per hour when you are traveling on a highway. But, it is very important for you to know what feels right for you and what allows you to ease into the zone.

Some of my patients need to have their energy level accelerated while others benefit from slowing down a bit.

Visualize a zone experience now and take note of the pace that feels right and works best for you. You will notice that your breathing and your physical movements feel comfortable when you discover this right speed.

Finding Your Balance

An idea that is closely related to your optimal energy level is the concept of not getting too high or too low. While the zone is often described as a kind "high," if you allow yourself to become too excited, you may find it difficult to get into this desired state of mind.

Similarly, if you get too low or too down on yourself and let yourself slip into an emotional valley, you will find it impossible to perform well.

There are a few mental techniques that seem to remind my patients of the importance of staying grounded. One of my patients, a professional golfer used to imagine that he was the human version of the flat line that you sometimes see on medical devices. Picturing this image helped him to stay calm and level during tournaments. The flat line image was important for him, since he used to have huge emotional swings during matches when he first came to see me.

Another patient who was a long distance runner used to imagine that he was running a perfectly level boardwalk, even if he was climbing a hill or descending into a valley.

A mid level manager, who frequently found himself in the midst of corporate, political storms, would go into his office and simply pretend that he was out fishing on a rough day. He would remind himself to take a few deep breaths and to find his "sea legs," when he was faced with unpleasant office conflicts. Recalling the image of himself fishing in some rough weather helped him to stay centered when office politics would rear its ugly head.

See if one of the images described in this section helps you find your center and your sense of balance. Feel free to create and utilize an image of your own. Some people like to use skiing, surfing, skating or rollerblading.

How To Remove Any Barriers That Are Keeping You From Entering The Zone

Occasionally, people do not know what is preventing them from getting into the zone. While it is useful to know what is getting in your way, sometimes people can solve this riddle by going through this exercise.

Simply imagine that you are walking on a path and suddenly you encounter a huge boulder which is blocking the route you wanted to take on your journey.

Now, you are not certain how this barrier got there, but you have a number of choices and options.

You can climb over it.

You can dig a hole and go under it.

You can find a sledgehammer or some dynamite and break it apart.

You can back away and collect your thoughts.

You can search for another path.

You can ask someone for help moving the boulder or for advice on another route.

You can sit on the boulder for a while and see if you discover a solution.

You can take a nap, sleep on it and perhaps you will find a solution in your dream.

The point is that no matter what the barrier is, your human spirit, intelligence and creativity can help you to find the help or solution you need to get past it.

Place Yourself In
A Comfortable Cocoon

Some of my patients have described the zone as feeling like a cocoon of concentration. And some of you know what it is like to feel that you are tuning out all distractions and totally focused on what you are doing and enjoying. I am actually frequently in this kind of state of mind as I write this book.

I am not thinking about the next chapter or the previous one. My fingers are doing their job. My house is quiet and there are no internal or external distractions. I am in a pleasant, safe comfortable and enjoyable vacuum, where I can easily lose track of time.

In your imaginary vacuum, you can feel what it is like to do things at varying speeds and at different levels of intensity. Your mind and your body are in perfect sync in your own universe. There is no external pressure—just you and your body.

Once you get comfortable, you can start to reintroduce whatever elements you would like to include in this safe and comfortable place. So, you can bring in your favorite person or persons, your favorite weather or your favorite music.

Or, you can elect to remain in your personal chamber all by yourself. For many people, the zone is this kind of cocoon. Create yours and see how it feels to you. Other people seem to thrive on the energy between themselves and others. People can be part of your cocoon. You will learn more about this idea when you learn the next technique described in this book.

Managing People

Some of the top performers and top achievers who have come to talk to me have had issues and concerns about managing fans, media, various publics, family, and people in the audience who are observing them. Handling your concerns about what other think about you is an important issue for people who want to enter the zone and perform their best. It is essential that you understand your own psychological makeup where this issue is concerned. The mental images you choose should fit with who you are and what gets you comfortable where other people are concerned.

It seems to me that you have a few options here. For instance, if you are someone who thrives on a large crowd, you may want to visualize lots of energized people cheering you on. This image can work very well for people who love being the center of attention and who love playing to the crowd.

Some people thrive on a hostile crowd and they love the idea of showing them up, winning them over or defying them in some way. A trial lawyer I worked with loved the challenge of trying to win over a jury that was not on his side at the start of a case.

Others like to imagine that they are performing to please one special person in their life. Some of my patients have pretended that their inner coach is watching their performance. This is a great technique if your inner coach was someone who was involved with coaching you in some way. One baseball player I worked with always would imagine that his dad was in the stands watching him on the field.

Some people do best by simply focusing on the task at hand. A high jumper I coached tuned out everything and everyone before he would jump. He was concentrated on clearing the bar and on nothing else. It did not matter if one person was watching him or if ten thousand people were in the audience. He was "a man with a mission." An executive who was nervous about public speaking took some of the pressure off of herself by trying to communicate with every single person in the audience. She felt that her anxiety would be alleviated if she viewed her speech as an opportunity to connect with other individuals.

Another executive who was quite shy did better at his public speaking by knowing his material very well, and the content of his talk very well. He found that practicing his speech to the point where he had it almost memorized allowed him to be quite comfortable when he got up to the podium. I have counseled a few stand-up comics. Some seem to like to feel very connected with an audience and they enjoy being quite spontaneous. Others perform in the zone by relying on a well-written and very well rehearsed routine.

Again, what you decide to visualize where the crowd is concerned has a lot to do with your own personality. If one approach is not working, be open to experimenting with other mental images. Many people who enter therapy seek it so they can manage interpersonal issues and their relationships with others more effectively. Sometimes, this is not an easy task. I have addressed the issue of managing people and relationships in many of my weekly newspaper columns. My wife who is trained as a therapist and now manages more than a hundred people and I frequently discuss strategies for handling complicated interpersonal matters. It is not always easy or simple. People can be quite complicated and confusing at times. Sorting out how you can manage people to allow yourself to enter the zone may require introspection and a willingness to experiment a lot. If one approach is working, stay with it. If it does not seem to help, try another one.

Find The Zone
Within You

Close your eyes and breathe deeply. Inhale the present and let go of the past and the future. Also, let go of negativity, self-doubt and any anxiety you might have. Breathe in calmness, confidence, focus and hope. Release negative energy, thoughts and ideas and absorb and embrace inspirational and positive feelings and memories.

Then count down slowly from one hundred to one. As you do this, at some point, and at some number, you will discover a very comfortable feeling.

I don't know if you will find it at ninety three or at fifty six. But you will discover your internal zone or your zone gear.

The number which houses your zone experience is very special. You can link this number and the counting exercise to entering the zone.

Use this simple technique to locate the zone within you. Many of my patients use this exercise several times a day.

You're Still Standing

Plenty of people have difficulty entering the zone because they have a fear of failing. This fear can paralyze people and can prevent them from reaching their potential.

However, once a person can visualize failing and can recognize in a deep and profound way that they will still be standing and that they will be okay, they usually start to let go of or overcome their fear of not doing well.

So, take a minute now to imagine that you perform poorly, lose, choke, embarrass yourself, and that you disappoint people whose opinion you really care about. Consider this situation in great detail and then notice that after it is happens, it can pass, and you will still be standing, and your life will go on.

Once you can face your deepest fears and be okay with it, you begin to convince your mind and your body that you will still be standing. You reduce your anxiety, build your confidence and free yourself up to enter the zone more often.

Taking Risks

Now that you know something about your ability to survive and to move ahead, it is important that you understand that the zone is not a frightened or a scared place. It is a place where you are comfortable and ready to take some risks and experiment a bit. In fact, the challenge or the adventure is precisely the thing that moves people into the zone.

When you think about being adventurous and about taking chances, you may want to view getting into the zone or being in the zone as being like a fishing trip.

Now, if you want to catch fish, you have to put at least one fishing line in the water. Sometimes, you may want to place several lines in the water. And when your line is in the water, you never knew what you might catch. You might catch a shark or a bluefish or a sailfish. But the adventure begins when you place your line in the ocean.

Like going fishing, the zone is a mental state where are you feel free, playful and eager to enjoy what you are involved in. If you are reluctant to take some chances, you are probably still fearing failure. Remember, there really are no failures in life. There are only successful experiences and learning experiences.

Where the zone and risk taking are concerned, sometimes I treat people who are taking too many risks and who are not relaxed and focused. They are putting too many different lines in the water at once and they tend to lack the focus that is a prerequisite for entering the zone. If you fall into this category, you may need to rein yourself in a bit and use the focusing exercise mentioned earlier on a regular basis. Try to get a little better at doing just one thing at a time. The cocoon technique might also be helpful for you as will the relaxation procedures described earlier in this guide.

Observing Yourself

Now, I know you bought this book because you want to perform better at something. Or, perhaps you purchased it to perform better at several tasks or activities.

And obviously, there is nothing wrong with wanting to do perform better. However, some people fail to perform well because they actually want success too badly and too immediately. Frequently, their ego is quite intertwined with their performance. That is, if they have a bad performance, they view themselves as bad or worthless and they also feel that others view them this way too. Here is a technique for removing some of your ego from your performance, and for detaching and disconnecting your self-worth from your accomplishments.

Close your eyes and take some nice deep breaths. And spend a little time watching yourself doing something you love. Begin watching yourself close up and then gradually increase the distance between your observing self and your performing self. You might imagine that you are a spectator in the stands or in the audience rather than yourself.

And notice what it feels like to have a little more physical and emotional distance from your own actions. You will probably feel very differently about yourself when you observe yourself in this manner. Even professional athletes whose livelihood depends on their performance have enjoyed this exercise. The idea is to gain a little distance, clarity and perspective about your performance and to not let it define you or your self-worth. Doing this will allow you to feel more relaxed and it will make it easier for you to enjoy, experiment and take risks.

Angels Can Fly, Because They Take Themselves Lightly

Many of you will find it easier to enter the zone if your mindset includes some levity, humor or lightness. For many people, a serious and intense approach is a barrier for getting into the zone.

Finding a way to enjoy the challenge that you are facing will allow you to enter the zone. Moreover, bringing a playful and curious spirit with you will increase the likelihood that you will get into the zone.

There is usually something that you can enjoy, learn, discover or have some fun with if you begin with the intent of finding a way to have some pleasant feelings with whatever challenge you are about to face.

So, take a moment to identify something that you can have some fun with your next performance or your next big event. Approach it with the playful curiosity of a child.

For example, you may be nervous about playing a tennis match. But, you can replace some or all of your nervousness with some curiosity about what the venue will be like and what the people might be like. Maybe, you will run into an old friend there.

Remember, you want to activate your playful, curious, risk taking side of your brain. You want to utilize the right part

91

of your mind that I discussed earlier in this book. Your curiosity and playfulness will go a long way to help to reduce any anxiety that you might have about performing well.

Interestingly, when I interview a new patient, I always ask them what they do for fun or what they enjoy in their lives. This question usually surprises them, but it helps me to understand them better. If a person can not identify any hobby, sport, pastime or avocation which gives them joy, I know that it will be harder for them to find a way to feel better about themselves and to enter the zone.

I really can not emphasize enough how important it is for you to find a way to love and enjoy your challenges and to live a life that is filled with a lot of enjoyment and fun.

Anchor Your Thoughts, Feelings, Memories, And Experiences In Your Favorite Object

Now you can pick up the object you focused on earlier in this guide and take a little time to associate all the useful feelings, memories, experiences, sensations, ideas, attitudes and behaviors that you find helpful with this item.

You will probably be amazed at all the pleasant and positive feelings you can easily recall and easily re-experience. It probably feels quite pleasant to you.

And from now on, whenever you hold this object in your hand or simply imagine the item, you will be able to recall and utilize the skills you have learned in this book to move yourself into the zone whenever you want to.

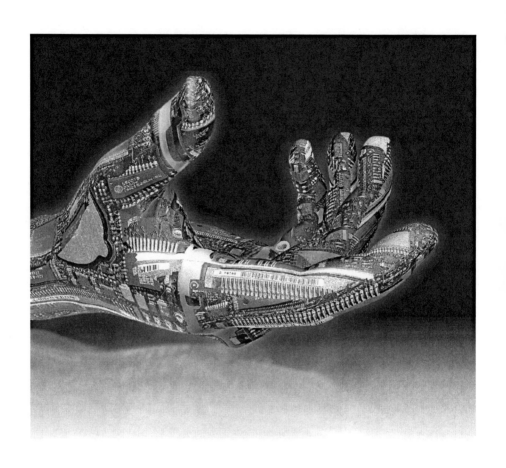

Three Scripts For Getting Into The Zone When The Pressure Is On

Many of you who purchased this book will find yourself in situations where you need to get into the right frame of mind to perform well—in a hurry.

Perhaps you are asked to unexpectedly speak or write on a topic that is somewhat foreign to you. Maybe you have to give a presentation to a client who is quite disenchanted with your firm. You may be waiting to interview with a perspective employer. Or, you may be an athlete who is asked to come through in the clutch or in a critical situation.

Now, lots of people find that one of the methods in this book gets their mind into the right place. If you have discovered one that works well for you, use it as often as you like.

Here are a few other popular scripts that patients of mine have used to get into the zone. These narratives are examples of how you can combine a few of the techniques to get your mind and body into the zone. Give these a try and see if you like them.

1

Imagine that you are sitting close to a beautiful campfire. You can see the beautiful shades of orange and yellow. And you are sitting close enough to it to see the grey and white pieces at the bottom of the fire. You can also feel the fire's heat and its energy as it warms every part of your body.

And as you enjoy the fire, you breathe deeply and you feel that you are not only absorbing its heat, but you are also internalizing some its energy, power and heat.

This energy warms your muscles and it fills your mind with strength, power and confidence. Now you can take all that you have absorbed and use it for whatever you want to and whatever you need to.

2

When the pressure is on, have a consultation with your inner coach. You know, who you spent time with earlier in this book. Just imagine that they are with you at your side. You can probably recall how they would handle the challenge that is facing you. And you can remember what they might say to you to encourage you, given what you need to accomplish right now.

You can also remember quite clearly how they would look at you and how they might hug you or give you a reassuring pat on your back or on your shoulder.

And you can never forget their eyes, their smile and the way they helped you to believe in yourself when you were faced with a challenge or an obstacle of some kind.

Well, you probably feel like they are with you right now, so you can feel quite confident that you are not alone in facing whatever is in front of you at this moment.

So, move ahead with great confidence and with a great belief in yourself and in your abilities.

3

What's the toughest thing you have ever done in your life? Was it climbing a mountain? Was it writing a book? How about passing an exam? How about learning to ride a bike or get over your fear of the ocean? Maybe you quit smoking. Maybe you lost weight. Perhaps you had to heal from the death of a loved one.

Well, those tough experiences are what build character and self-confidence. So, it is always useful to reminisce about a time in your life when the going got really tough and you got really tough and got going.

You never gave up. You were resilient like a rubber ball. You persevered when you had to keep plugging away.

Knowing that you succeeded at something really hard is something you can revisit when you want to elevate your confidence and your performance at almost anything.

Now that you are familiar with many of the techniques for entering the zone, I want you to take a moment to reflect on what you have really enjoyed so far. Maybe you liked the music. Maybe you enjoyed the playfulness. Perhaps you got in touch with a wonderful memory. Some of you will discover some confidence you didn't know you had in you. Getting in touch with your optimal energy level may be very meaningful for you. I am certain that lots of you enjoyed your visit with your inner coach.

By the way, as you practice your mental techniques, you will see that sometimes one part is more important to you than others. For example, at times, the relaxation piece will be most useful. Other times, you may derive the most benefit from your inner coach or from your recalling an optimal performance of yours from some time ago. Sometimes, the levity or humor will be the key for you.

You are not a machine. You are a dynamic human being who is changing and hopefully growing all the time.

Remember, as I mentioned earlier, different challenges will require you to shift into different mental gears. Experimenting and using some trial and error are all part of the activities you need to be open to in order to find your best pathways to your zone.

Some Creative Techniques For Entering The Zone

For those of you who want a longer, step by step, approach for entering the zone which incorporates most of the ideas of the various one minute exercises the list that follows ought to be quite helpful.

This list below includes all of the techniques mentioned in this guide. You can use any of the one minute techniques, or you can mix and match these techniques:

Enjoy Your Favorite Music

Smile

Focus

Stay In The Here And Now

A Simple Way To Relax Your Mind

How To Relax Your Body In One Minute

Move Your Mind To The Right Path

Take A Mental Vacation

Make Contact With Nature

Build Your Confidence

Dream A Glorious Dream

Discover Your Right Energy
Level

Finding Your Balance

Remove Any Barriers That Are
Keeping You From Entering
The Zone

Place Yourself In A
Comfortable Cocoon

Managing People

You're Still Standing

Risk Taking

Observing Yourself

Angels Can Fly Because They Take Themselves Lightly

Anchor Your Thoughts, Feelings, Memories And Experiences For example, you can simply relax your mind and your body and then listen to your favorite music.

Or, you can find something to smile about and then have a visit with your inner coach. You can take a one minute mental vacation on the beach and then make contact with nature by sitting next to a beautiful camp fire in the woods. You may decide to find your right energy level and then revisit a perfect performance that you have delivered in the past. You can pick up your favorite object and dream your big dream. You can hold your favorite object in your hand, listen to some music and wake up your playful side. You can move your mind to the right path and then explore your big dream. You can experiment with relaxing your mind and then your body. Or, you can quiet your body and then your mind.

A professional golfer rediscovered his swing's tempo by relaxing his mind and his body and then listening to his favorite Beatles tune.

A tennis player found that he could enter the zone by waking up his playful side before a match.

A boxer who I counseled found that he could develop the right kind of aggressiveness by listening to "Eye Of The Tiger" and then making contact with nature by imagining that he was, in fact, a tiger.

Over the years, I have been amazed at how creative people have been when it comes to using these mental techniques. I would encourage you to experiment a bit and find what approach you enjoy the most.

Some of the people I have counseled record their own narratives using any or all of the techniques in this list. Here is an example of how it might sound.

I'm feeling pretty tense. I think I will put on some of my favorite music. Then it will be good for me to recall the time I laughed so hard I could hardly breathe.

Now I am going to hold that beautiful rock that I found in the ocean last year.

To ground myself in the present, I am going to spend a few seconds just focusing on the second hand of my watch. A couple of deep breaths and a few times of clenching my fists will help to calm my mind and my body and remove any uncomfortable feelings. And as I get comfortable, I can recall that wonderful vacation I took last year. That beach in the Caribbean was outstanding. I can remember everything about it right now. I really loved scuba diving down there. It was like being in another world. I went deeper than I had ever gone before on my last dive. I was swimming at a very comfortable pace under the water. I didn't feel like I was working hard at all. It was so easy and so much fun. I got a little scared once or twice, but I challenged myself in small steps and my confidence grew the deeper I went in the water.

It is really fun to take myself to this nice place. Whenever I hold that wonderful rock in my hand I can revisit these wonderful feelings. And I can take these memories and these sensations to whatever I want to in my work life or my play life. Now I feel comfortable. I feel like I am In The Zone.

Use Your Zone Experience For Whatever You Want

And now, you can use whatever you liked and enjoyed in this book to accomplish whatever you want to accomplish. Some of you will use this method for sports. Others will apply this tool to your work life. Parents can teach this technique to their kids. There is really no limit to the application of these techniques.

Be sure to share your zone experiences with me. You can reach me at: info@stayinthezone.com.

About The Author

Jay P. Granat, Ph.D. is a psychotherapist with twenty-five years of experience. He has shown thousands of people from all walks of life how to get into the zone. Dr. Granat writes a weekly newspaper column on sports psychology, sports, humor, parenting, stress management, psychotherapy, relationships, nostalgia, marriage counseling and family issues.

He has authored articles for professional journals and developed a half a dozen self-help programs. He has appeared in many media outlets including Good Morning America, *The New York Times*, The British Broadcasting Company, The Canadian Broadcasting Company, The Associated Press, ESPN Radio, *ESPN Magazine, Golf Digest, Tennis Magazine, The Iowa Golfer* and *Executive Golfer.*

He writes a weekly column for three newspapers, and has authored articles for professional journals, and developed a half dozen self-help programs including: How To Get In The Zone And Stay In The Zone With Sport Psychology And Self-Hypnosis; How To Lower Your Golf Score With Sport Psychology And Self-Hypnosis; 101 Ways To Break A Hitting a Slump With Sport Psychology Techniques; How To Conquer

Test Anxiety and Long-Term Weight Control. Many of these programs are available at www.StayInTheZone.com.

A former university professor, he received his Ph.D. and M.A. from The University of Michigan. Dr. Granat has lectured at some of America's largest corporations including Hyatt, Schering Plough, Paine Webber and MFS.

He is the Founder of: www.StayInTheZone.com and can be reached at: info@stayinthezone.com or at 888-580-ZONE.

Praise for:

Get Into The Zone In Just One Minute;
21 Simple Techniques To Improve Your Performance

1. Are you an athlete who wants to perform better?
2. Are you a parent or coach of an athlete who is choking when the pressure is on?
3. Are you a sales person who wants to deliver more compelling presentations?
4. Are you a manager who wants to teach your staff how to reach their potential?
5. Would you like to learn a simple strategy for managing stress, anger and frustration quickly and efficiently?
6. Would you like to discover a simple way to tap into your confidence?
7. Would you like to be calm instead of feeling overwhelmed?
8. Are you interested in reaching your fullest potential?
9. Are you tired of performing poorly at work or at your favorite sport?
10. Would you like to learn how to get into the zone quickly and stay there?

If you answered "yes" to any or all of these questions, this book is probably the right one for you.

"YOU'RE BOOK IS FANTASTIC...HOPE TO HEAR FROM YOU SOON ON ANYTHING NEW!!!...THANKS KARL"

– Karl Mallock, professional bowler

Dr. Granat:

I don't know if you remember me or not. I ordered your CD back in March, early April. My son has been listening to the CDs and we have definitely seen an improvement in his game. He seems more confident and less stressed when things don't go his way. I am grateful.

I've been so pleased with the CD that I recommended it to a co-worker whose son goes to a different high school than mine. His son suffers from the same issues as my son. I was telling him what a difference we have seen in our son's attitude and performance and he is considering ordering the CD for his son as well. Thank you again.

– Cindy Taylor

Hello Dr. Granat!

I have been using the 2 volume cd for about 3 months now and it's awesome what it has done for me. It might be irrelevant, but I race downhill mountain biking and it has helped me achieve a higher level of confidence when coming down the mountain and overcoming obstacles I couldn't before. I was wondering how much is each personal session and how the appointments are set with you. I'm racing the U.S. Open this year and I'd like some counseling before the event, which is on May 28th. I'd also like some info about your seminars; I live in NJ so I'd like to assist to some of them. Well Dr., thanks for your time and I hope to hear from you soon!

– Victor Giusfredi

CPSIA information can be obtained at www.ICGtesting.com
Printed in the USA
BVOW080035240113

311446BV00002B/102/P